MASS

ROBERT LUNDQUIST

www.farwestpress.com

First Edition

ISBN 979-8-9913506-3-1

Printed in the United States of America

Cover Art & Photos by Parker Love Bowling

Contents

ON HOLDING THE INERTIA OF THE
WORLD:
An introduction to Robert
Lundquist's *MASS* by David Erdos

PART I: MASS...13

PART II: GRAVITATIONAL WAVES.................63

PART III: EQUIVALENCE 67

PART IV: Uncertainty A..79

PART V: Uncertainty B..93

Acknowledgements

Thanks to the editors of *The London Magazine*, *Unpolished Poems*, *Mu Magazine*, *The International Times*, and the Serbian magazine *Libartes*. And with great appreciation to Nazare Magaz, Heathcote Ruthven, Ana Seferovic, Mersiha Bruncevic, Suzy Feay, Ithamar Handelman-Smith, and David Erdos.

ON HOLDING THE INERTIA OF THE WORLD

An introduction to Robert Lundquist's *MASS*

Just as William Blake evaluated the price of experience, so does the American poet Robert Lundquist ruminate on its weight. His new epic poem, *Mass*, which you are about to read and encounter on all vital levels, is a philosophical and spiritual treatise on the impact of the senses in relation to the forces that stir and inspire them. It is also deeply felt poetic reflection on the losses and gains engendered by moving through a particular landscape, fused from both the poet's childhood and successive stages, alongside the world in general.

Written in what appears to be prose (apart from one Beat-like section), in each sentence an image elevates description into the twin realms of dream and action, via a state that has been described on the Exberliner Books website as one of 'ecstatic compassion.' The phrase 'chapter and verse' also achieves true resonance here as the alignment of each thought and reaction form solid and independent stanzas, paragraphs and episodes, each aiming to occupy and influence the readers' interpretation, while at the same time forming part of a far greater quest: chiefly, to unify (as Einstein did) all true 'fields' of experience.

The pertinence of the opening quote from the physics lesson is demonstrated by what Lundquist presents us with: a series of poetic vibrations emanating from the same source, or theme, with each wave of recognition dedicated to understanding the weight of man's war with the world. To what extent does our presence on the planet and the life we have carved from it affect the natural order, and just how deep do our impressions and indentations reach on the fouled and still sacred earth? Lundquist uses second-person singular to address his own motivations and the general reader as a whole, an ideal device in that it allows for both artistic detachment and a fuller consideration of attitudes, events, and perspective, opening out one person's sensibility for everyone else to now share.

The correlation between entries is for you to navigate. How each numbered section relates to its sibling is a matter of style, theme, and subject. They are experiments, vibrations and variations, as if each event could be viewed through the eye of the needle by the eyes of an insect, amphibian, or marsupial. And indeed, there is a sense of flight to these words, as the poet's form hovers between states, drawing inspiration and horror from outcomes as changeable as the wind and as graced as the light from a star. *Mass*'s protagonist(s) is faced with a series of choices and decisions, while being reminded that any decision made is part of a far greater process, to do with the notion and act of creation itself, both in terms of what appears on the page and of what formed the pieces of the planet that holds that page together in the first place. Line after line comments on that which has preceded and will succeed it, marrying these entries, epistles and miniature gospels, with the science that exists behind them, to create a quantum masterpiece, with each poem page forming innumerable versions of the same seven universes, or states of being. Conversely, the one story of the poet's experience and relationship with the world around and the events encountered within it undergoes over a hundred special experiments, designed to test his found theories and to cultivate their own form of growth. Something as specific and grounded as the need to evaluate what has happened and is happening within the act of living at any moment, is also able to invoke the more abstract need to adapt, transform, and evolve into a form of consciousness capable of seeing and meeting all possible permutations of self *at all times*. The weight of responsibility when divided by spiritual worth, raised to the power of poetry and perception creates the equation of *Mass*.

Lundquist's journey has been a special one, and this is a special poem. The son of sanatorium-bound mother and a LAPD detective who mostly worked narcotics underground, leaving Xs on the calendar as to when the phone could be answered and the times they could leave the house, and who on one occasion arrested Lenny Bruce (a fact the poet has felt ashamed of all his life), Lundquist was saved by his displaced German grandmother. A teenage spell in a Zen Buddhist Zendo led to his poetic awakening and saved his life. At the age of twenty-two, he was a celebrated member of the renaissance in literature occurring in Santa Cruz, California. He was published in *The Nation*, *The Paris Review*, *Poetry Now*, the celebrated *Kayak*, *Quarry West*, and *Rolling Stone*. In Santa Cruz he befriended the American Beat poet William Everson. A subsequent period of early alcoholism led to a period of poverty and homelessness, before at twenty-nine he recovered and began a series of long-form poems featured by Raymond Carver in his literary magazine *Quarry West*. This second flowering was interrupted by Lundquist's own choice to stop writing. After reading John Ashbery, Paul Celan, Edmond Jabès, Hilda Morely, and the Language poets, Lundquist felt a need to set aside writing in favor of reading and learning. He had no idea this pause would last thirty years.

As narrative poetry dominated the American stage— only to be interrupted by Morely, the Black Mountain poets, Ashbery, and the Language poets—Lundquist began to read, take notes, and undergo psychoanalysis, the beginning of his thirty-year journey to become an analyst and recover from his own trauma. A solitary freedom led to a life path whose intimate details can be felt as you read *Mass*. Lundquist used the decades away from his writing to train as a psychoanalyst, to assist the disadvantaged, and to help those unable to cope with life's many challenges. This mastering of everyday intention and unknown motivation would prove to be an invaluable asset to his writing and sensibility. By living through extremes, true balance can be achieved; the impact and weight of Lundquist's experiences that informed the early work, considered through his decades of study, now afford the later work a sense of star-sourced wisdom.

Analysis, illness, and wisdom are all poetic in aspect, albeit in vastly different ways, and it is only now, all these years later, that the cumulative effect of experience can be quantified. Whether putting pen to paper or not, Robert Lundquist continued to write with the heart, mind, and soul, accumulating experiences that have led to the work we can now enjoy and fully engage with. His first book, *After Mozart* (*Heroin on 5th Street*), was published by Robert Montgomery's New River Press in 2018. Now, after nearly four years of hibernation, shared with the rest of the world, he emerges with a radically different statement, the shimmer and sheen of a mature artist reflecting on the strange new fields he has sewn, and peopled by the wilting and emergent mind-flowers of those both suffering and recovering from their own private wars with the earth.

There is a sense of therapy to *Mass* as you read it— felt in its need to guide, minister to, and advise both poet and audience—as well as something otherworldly. Life is lifted. Bridges seek the edge of light. Mountains strive to reach the sea. Trees and roads bear witness. Skies comment, and all around is an animation of person and place that makes the form of this book as malleable as the imagination allows. It is a collection of psalms and a need to build new cathedrals. It is both invocation and the search for a private demon, or God. It is every possible man and each enveloping woman. It is indiscriminate sunlight, and the cities and sin found in shadow. It is age and the baby. It is the appraisal of what the spirit makes of the flesh.

There are lines to surprise and lines here to haunt you. There is proof, refutation, denials and dreams, promises. All leave their marks as they pass like light through your prism, or sun-masked moons in your orbit. Each phrase as you feel it is a special star behind clouds. What *Mass* leaves you with, more than anything else, is a longing, for both your life to change and for a planet that is as alive to your touch as you'd wish. The fact that it is, and that man-unkind cannot see it, is part of the tragedy that confines us, until at last we can see. Poems like this point the way. It is not for me to distract you, which is why this introduction does not quote, or tell you 'the story.' You are the story. And as you become it, you will, like Lundquist, start to carry the weight and gain of the world. Robert Lundquist lifts you, along with Nazare Magaz, his beloved life-partner (whose painting appears above). They take you back through twin suns, to the One.

David Erdos

London
27 July 2022

Like the mass on a spring in the animation at the right, a vibrating object is moving over the same path over the course of time. Its motion repeats itself over and over again. [. . .] The time it takes to complete one back-and-forth cycle is always the same amount of time.
—from *The Physics Classroom*

Constant fluctuations in energy can spontaneously create mass as if out of thin air.
—-Nazare Magaz

If you think you understand quantum mechanics, you don't understand quantum mechanics.
—Richard Feynman

The entanglement of two particles is like you have a pair of dice. Three is rolled on one die and three is rolled on the other. If one die shows six, the other shows six, the other always shows six. And the same number always comes up on both dice.
—Anton Zellinger

*To pass through pain and not know it
A car door slamming in the night
To emerge on an invisible terrain*
—John Ashbery, from "A Wave"

PART I: MASS

1.

It is in the interest of the right question. What needs
pinning down. Perhaps the inside of a moment at
rest. Perhaps the part of the idea missing. The ice
slips out to sea, slices a ship in half. Always prepare
for the possibility no one survives. Wait for sunset,
wait for the last one to enter. It will be dark: find
your way by the light around its rim. When it
springs out, starts to dance, give it the floor until
the applause. As bars close down for the night,
rumors begin. Privately, other things could be said,
things unlikely mentioned because a leak in the
conversation, the strings attached.

2.

While no bigger than a leaf, while falling from nests,
the tails of thoughts tumble in the bright air through
phrases like *don't lead with your chin, don't jab off
your back foot*, because you think it is in the numbers,
and it is, at least, it is eventually. What you don't
understand is to first lie, lie a lot, until somebody
believes your story, then you can talk about the
numbers. As the left side of reason lights up like
a Christmas tree, you think, *there should be no
problems*; however, cars stop for trains no longer in
service. A walk home takes forever. A casserole stays
warm overnight in the fridge. The ice in your glass
never melts and your last breath finished.

3.

Previously, there were only dry leaves breaking under your feet. Now, with the echoes of clouds about to rain, retreat into a small village and place a guard inside each doorway. Grab onto the horse, the cop with the reins in his hands looking down at you looking up at him, and under birds forming a perfect wave, kick the beast, because anyone can see the air not just inside of it.

1.

Your guess is as good as the next. Your side of the
equation simple enough until you factor you will
not see it coming; it will always have its back to you;
without a name the land stretching to the horizon
is just baked earth. What you cannot tell the others,
water is a thing of the past unless the stick in front
of you bows down and there is no mistake. So you
walk in circles ahead of everyone, far enough that
no one can see your arms and legs; no one can see
whether or not it is time to pray. Without a bird in
the sky, your only plan, to stretch the circumference
your absence spins, a sky gathering this day's tears the
moment before the sun sets, the rains begin.

2.

The ropes to cross the rivers all belong to you,
and you have no idea if the last strands will hold.
Thankfully, the light remains around the edge. Will
you mend the hooves when stones lodge in a soft
foot? Your sense of direction, the tips of your fingers
inside a world losing its sun, yet revolving around
it? How you will keep your feet on the ground is
anyone's guess, and the money is not with you: the
bet is on the strings wrapping around your legs,
dragging you into space while your loved ones, close
behind, have to guess which gas to breathe and
when.

3.

Through your skin, flowers bloom on a hillside
scattered with the memories of which leaves fall,
and when, as a kindness, for no reason, drift out of
reach in a gentle wind. Still, with no one to hold
onto in the coldest of nights, tiny blossoms wait
patiently for the smallest gesture, like a hand gently,
tenderly, touching your cheek. When you finally
rest, the softest chair on which to stretch your legs
moves beside you. A rug settles inside the pasture.
The paintings at the base of each tree show various
families in conversation. This is your family now,
flowers and stars spinning over you, a bouquet of
many days and many nights lying alone, beneath the
smallest of strings, beneath light.

1.

You are only here until the roses bloom, until you notice a second skin folding like ribbon through your dreams of one last embrace. To accept this is to accept the past and all who perished along with your wish to grace each child who stayed to march beside you. And you did. As well as those living inside the darkest thoughts of who will finally lie in order to hide the truth that no one made it to the end where leaves fall to open the sky, grow back in to close the sky once more.

2.

You stand here, appearing, disappearing, delicately
separating flesh from flowers on a bed of moss
you cling to, like dry ice sticking to the hand of a
child. When you turn to face the wind, you are the
log floating next to the bridge you walk over each
morning, dust and time spreading through your
leaves. As winter approaches, you feel your stems
breaking. If it is up to you, you will hide inside the
shadows that separate you from all who traveled
under a cold sun, waiting for the earth to part, the
water to spray from pools just beneath the surface
you have come to depend upon.

3.

It is not up to you who will survive, who will follow
you past the meadows to the cliffs you are about to
descend. Who will follow are those who listen to the
right wind at the right time while hearing your voice
when the wind dies down. And as the wind dies
down, you become another source of knowledge.
As a source of knowledge, you study the paintings
in the rooms of the caves in which you wander. It
will take time to understand the sunlight gathering
the shadows filling in the drawings on each wall. As
you look closely, between the cracks and the lines
of paint, it seems like something between light and
dark gathers all of the hooves running towards you,
pounding the rocks on the banks below.

1.

In a moment, you, your sister, the elk in the middle of the road, all against the windshield of your car. The tiny balls of glass roll through your clothes, your skin, your cheeks as you stagger into the weeds. Your thoughts spin you around a forest you cannot see. You attempt to rouse your sister from a certain sleep. The ribs of the buck rise on the hood of your car. Somewhere between the fender of the car and the gravel lining the highway you try to stand; your sister, now on her knees, begins to vomit. Another car, turning the corner, slams on its brakes too late; the ribs of the buck again rise, moonlight holding on to your sister cracks open like an egg without letting go.

2.

You would think all's well that ends well. It's true: the road arrives peacefully to its end. The mountains do their best to find the sea. For all of the right reasons, the sun rises at the same time, and most everyone wakes as usual. Still, there are those of us who remain weary, even as the leaves fall in the wind and the breath between us keeps us warm. No one but you wants to solve the problem surrounding the ledge: a particular edge moving forward, jutting out, hoping to become a cliff. You want to stand here, alone, looking up at the sky, not just for you, but everyone who turns too wide, too fast.

3.

Right now, everyone at their window tries to make
sense of the skins on the side of the road. You are
waiting until the difference between yesterday
disappears, until you forget the length of your car,
until the flesh seen through the blinds piles so high
the day turns to night. You think of all the birds
pouring their wings into the one sweet moment
where nothing that it is like to be comes to rest.
The very slopes you have come to call yourself
narrow the valleys in which you may need to hide.
You remember leading the way. You remember
your sister asking you to drive. The moon rises over
your fears and what you hope to keep to yourself.
You remember opening the door for her. You have
forgotten everything when asked who towed you
home.

1.

Here's what you should do: follow the road around your hill until the trees learn to stand inside the wind, the skin lying on the side of the road wearing your sister's dress covered in leaves. You wait for the patience to understand your face of indifference, the space holding your indiscretions stays behind you, and the lattice built to hold you leans away from the house you enter each night to dream whenever you can. When your sister arrives, she holds you tightly, together bracing against the wind, smelling her body for the last time. When she is almost gone, you stare at your hands still holding on to an animal resting in your own arms, struggling to breathe.

2.

You begin to trace what comes before you. The length of you cast out, reeled in, taken home to the box in which you keep a record of the work only done by hand. Like digging graves no one will ever see simply because of a lack of desire to pray or remember. Or because too much, already pale, put back to earth. Or, you leave behind what you need to carry when the weight of everything is on the side of the road, often limp, but closely watched, trying to raise a hand.

3.

All this folding in. Like sheets of waste. A car bent
over a car inside a sky bent over. But none of this
grabs the pin from the lapel. What keeps you going
is how you insure yourself harm. The steps that take
you there rest on the soft hands you bury. You forget
the day it begins, and the closer you are to it you try
tucking in the corners. So the sleeves haunt you as
the collars turn down. Anything arriving now may
or may not be solid. If you peel back the flesh, it will
center on the plate. You regret the bits and scraps
you have become. You guard your throat. You turn
around. What is ahead of you already happens;
the future stays at the door you will not open, still,
resuming each moment in the wind, the car in front
of you parks on the side of the cliff upon which you
stand, drives over.

1.

It certainly feels like it is moving towards you,
eventually walking beside you. You might want to
lean closer, see how it breathes, know if it is leaving
or coming back. Fortunately, your chest rises each
time you move towards its embrace. Each night
you wait for everything to close, wait until you no
longer see your hand in the dark, confident your
steps leave no trace. What you are like is still on its
way. You may weigh less. Paying attention to each
moment and lying down will help, help you to take a
necessary pause, getting up carefully.

2.

You are known as many things: a pile, a heap, a
cloud, the floor of the moon lit up each night by
a star. What is curious about before and after sags
together sometimes between light and dark hanging
upside down like a doe no longer in the forest, in
your garage. You, personally, will never stop, but you
will slow the fish swimming in your wake. Receding
carefully, into the near future, behind the trees and
rising up on your hind legs, you continue to follow
the right path where you see the lines drawn to
separate each lane, and then you cross.

3.

You are like new skin over a fresh wound, and you
need your trees more than ever to fence off the wind
that only leaves dust behind. You have been here
before, searching for water because someone finds
their thirst, and you know if only you can walk
far enough in the correct direction you will finally
return, take all their hands into yours, raise their
bodies over your shoulders and, while they hang on,
climb.

1.

Before your next breath and before the moss dries
between your shoulders as you hunch on all fours,
the elk rub antlers against your trees, and while gills
open and leaves fall, your wish, your hope for that
one moment to stop folding in whatever comes
next, fold in whatever is hunting you, hunting
everyone who drives home alone after the wheels, no
longer touching the ground, spin in the air, as if the
moment is traveling inside you, a cold wind so fast
cars stop, unable to pull over.

2.

Certainly, one of you must have known. If not from
each other, then someone else who understood how
to help, as when you first learned to stay warm when
you turned around and someone put skins over you,
leaving behind the fur for those in most need, fur
you could have used as you walked into the cold into
thick ice, fish swimming in circles ahead of you, as if
to guide you into the trees at the edge of the shore
with new fires building for you to lie beside as the
stars come out as you listen to everything moving,
carefully pulling out a piece of you burning.

3.

As your hand passes through you, you touch your
petals burnt around the edges, each passing cloud
bending sunlight as you walk over your hills,
through your trees, to a lake frozen with elk. The
ledge of your first step is buried here, covered with
moss. When you lift your foot, a car opens its
front door for you to climb in, your sister sitting
in the back seat laughing. You smile, you step in
to drive her home. This is your car, your hill, your
flowers, your first step. Rain and leaves fall in either
direction. She tells you she was supposed to be the
rocks that build your walls, stay despite the wind, the
same rocks that will build your home, build the sides
of the roads with broken glass, let in all the air she
used to breathe.

1.

So you huddle together, smoothing the ashes, setting aside the bones that did not burn. Very early in the day the sun sets inside you. You are not ready for the darkness that burrows in. Or the dream of waking up at the base of a tree, your hands tied behind you, a wagon approaching to take you back to *everything matters nothing stays*.

2.

What you hope to understand, despair to explain,
grips the patch of light cast out each night to hold
the bottom so the bottom stays, so that the flat
fish drag the beds of kelp fastened below the sides
turning you over to forget, turning you over the stars
falling behind you never see.

3.

The risks you take gather your roads for reasons only
found halfway up your hill, where your chairs, rugs,
flowers set in place your belief in the trails leading
away from drought, away from the broken arms and
legs, the skirts scattered in the center of the lane you
drive to remember the lines no one should cross,
even though you turn on your lights, signal twice,
stay up all night so moonlight stays.

1.

It is still inside of you: it's leather straps and steal
mask, though butterflies waft, and look! They are all
around the lemon tree, where the bushes wrap, bark
shaved by the rumps of bears, dark red wood under
a bright green canopy. The smallest bat barely seen,
with clouds inside the nests of bees, where the hole
is dug beneath a stream, because of leather straps
around your knees, your face encased in metal leaves.

2.

The straw is almost in the barn, in hay you will lie
on top of me, and because of all you said, between
the sores that coat your lips, around the time they
take you away, when crows stand upon the garbage
heap, and when the morning sun warms you, as if
your leather straps and metal jaws around the bit
protected me.

3.

And when you swam beyond the waves, beds of kelp
no longer in the sea, and what about the lambs laid
over you, the long weeks of winter and finally snow
sweeping over thorns that you must know, when I
say the last dinner was for him and not for you. Fur
burrows so quietly.

1.

The blinding sun answers this; the field cut down to
seed is your only chance to come home to rest, your
homage to begin ends, that and this; his elements
of style clasps all that straps your lips your neck, ties
back your hair, the face you hide but not its stare, the
mask you wake with, the strings you will never see
inside of you.

2.

Your steps swagger here languish there; your hands
applaud the swinging low and high from tree to tree,
the limbs broken against all that is said and done,
and when you do speak, speak of tender moments to
be kind, spill tenderness on everything.

3.

Charred, you went unnoticed at the bottom. You
neither moved nor remained at rest. But now
the straps are too tight; the belt around your face
unravels in the same place. Did you really need to do
this, keep your face hidden from view, keep yourself
at bay, when other members have stayed on, stayed
when all that is burning comes into view, burns
down, blows away.

1.

The moment you feel your eyes closing, your arms
reach for a new wheel to steer, the road which your
hands your fingers grab, the curve on which you lean
towards the next wreck, the next car warning you of
a hard ground you will need to smooth, the sides of
you still the hills whose streams run with fish leaping
far inside the nets between.

2.

But what about your face your face as if from stems
to bloom all desire looking back at the loops of
straps whose clasps close, open the moments your
eyes close your reach. You can think about this, but
don't imagine more than one mask for all to share.
The corners fold in fold over, pull you close to your
chest and whisper goodbye to a face looking back at
all that is possible that possibly remains.

3.

If you are to stay, stay in one place, beneath the
stream along the eucalyptus trees from which the
butterflies hang, hang from the corners turning in,
where only one life remains, borrows past the rest
of the day to watch the sky, the sun falling through
the course of one gaze whose sides cannot divide the
hills or caves where smoke dies down, where hooves
are cleaned.

1.

Growing older, you often stay in the shade,
conceding only enough light for us to follow.
Though we only exist in your imagination, living and
dying inside you, and though you flip us like a coin,
you never mean for us to trace the sounds you leave
behind, sounds inside the gas only you could prepare
us. Like a mother who marries too young, finally
leaving her own children behind to find a reason to
exist, you now believe you know exactly why you
are here: to be with each other, as we together look
inside the air that spreads over your trees, helping
the roots of younger leaves, roots we swore to keep
safe from the first time we spoke your name, when
you still found the time to take off the straps and let
us breathe.

2.

Slicing you thin seems to be an option you keep on
the table; your gills open and close when the hooks,
taken from your lips, fall over the rails into a sea
whose flowers are the beds on which you sleep. How
you expect more from yourself, lying there, twisting
the knife used against you, the knife used to take out
the large bones you know of but never understand
how they hold you together, your own firm meat,
grateful for any diversion, lifting the knife away from
your worst fear, separation; our hope remains the
same; the sea and the boats may take us further from
shore, but not from each other.

3.

You wanted to leave behind the fish you caught
earlier in the day when the sun set quietly like the
drawers you close before bed. For you, as for us,
it is a matter of staying out of sight, unavailable
to scrutiny, and you are able to hide what is most
important, us. We can never thank you enough. This
is the only reason we will make it back safely, why we
can finally rest, take back our face, listen to what was
said so long ago, only reaching us now.

1.

It is important to imagine the skins around you as
the heat clutches what will someday hatch beneath
you. It is important to imagine you and everyone
who follows you trapped inside cages with lights
on all night while whole flocks, outside, stare into
the rain, drown as they lift their beaks towards a sky
whose clouds wrap around your hill, your eggs too
cold to survive. So you wrap yourself tighter, with
new skins you find on the side of the road after you
learn which direction to cross, which direction water
and food still exist, the last of us finding shelter
inside the trees in which you stopped our bleeding.

2.

Inside the caves, while taking your hands away from the sticks still burning, smelling the smoke inside the small stones, you hide your last excuse, your words nestle against the walls until someone finds you gently rocking from side to side, the large rocks you promised to carry covering the holes in which you are last seen, the reasons to leave, the thin air as it disappears, and the stories you know are not true gathering our reasons to leave.

3.

Once you look squarely at the face you give us, the
face we learned to hide, once you take up the knife
to scrape away our scales you find no weight; what
stays does not breathe, casts itself beyond the loss
sealed in moments we do as you ask; never disturb
all of the pretense binding us to your repetitions
while in this faith, believing you will never die, that
you will create rarely read and rarely seen, create
what keeps and what cannot be saved.

1.

Towards the end, only the most devoted stay, still believe your main ideas will bring back our memories of the coldest lakes we crossed and why. We know now the fish pretend to float, so our lines will never bring them back. If we are to survive, we have to rise towards the sky accordingly, build our homes high on your hills, learn to drive on your roads winding to the top, careful never to disturb your flowers on your peaks, grateful your thorns protect us from predators larger than the beginning, middle, and end; starting over to learn a bit more than the time before, remember always, without the lakes and the ice over them, none of our coats will thicken; none of us will cross because none of us will remember the time of day the fog lifts to see the other side.

2.

To imagine we are finally on our own loosens our
teeth. You said the ice slips out to sea, slices a ship in
half, that antlers wash onto shore wrapped in plastic
bags. If we turn to kiss your cheek, we feel the hard
times that ruined your face. You seem to feel anxious
even by our approach. Sometimes, when someone
tells a lie, it is built on a previous truth. Like before
the lakes were here, before the fish broke the surface,
no one lived here. Yet bones float just below the
ice, cleaned of any meat. And before the sun sets
each night, someone seems to be watching, moving
carefully between the trees, waiting for us to sleep,
never showing his face.

3.

What rips open our heart, ruins the map leading
to our salvation, leading to where each skin begins,
perhaps leading to the front of you, to the face that
solves the following riddle: when we are the ones
who find the water no one else can see, how do we
survive when each of us is grabbed from behind,
taken into the trees? Something or someone is on
the move; perhaps it is the front of you waiting for
us to return, but perhaps it is just falling, knows
nothing about you, not even how you begin.

1.

While you stare out the windows in front of you,
tracing your thoughts to the beginning, assured of
the directions you travel, your desires softening like
cheese in a warm room, the pale side of which way
to slice your life sweats across the plate you offer to
no one, each car spinning under wheels no longer
gripping the moment each track was laid in front of
you.

2.

How we will recognize this, see the rest of us staying
close to the bottom, belongs to the time to get
there when the time to get there is more than just a
tantalizing glimpse of melted goodness. Fact is, we
know it will strike us suddenly, gills kissing the air as
boats leave for deeper water. What we do know is the
yeast grows, rises into the clouds, lifting the air for
the rest of us to enter.

3.

The dead hover on the side of the road. That we
know this and still offer our veins whenever blood
is needed is how we come to know you, how we
come to know ourselves, how we learn to land safely.
As the winds die down, feeling like husks scattered
over your hill, thin lines across your face trace what
is left of you, what is left of the hooks set in, and
the hooves cleaned, packed into boxes, loaded onto
trains. Nevertheless, after the rinds cross your knife,
and when the soured milk is poured again, you arrive
to claim all of you all of us all of our life in skins
between.

1.

It will be at night. The wings of birds heard inside
their cages. The trains that run inside you filled with
cattle. You change your appearance. Tack on slices of
breath. You remember the elk before and after. You
will not mention the floods, the excuses faster and
faster lifting your mask above a reason to rest; the
tears in your eyes forget the first turn around the first
hill, the lines you will cross, the ideas that helped,
the reasons you wake, the antlers in the trees, the ice
melting, the elk before and after, the floods, the skins
torn apart.

2.

You need to start a fire and all you have is wet
grass, fresh fish, the remains of elk, and the branch
continuing to bend towards water, all of which
provide a perception of simple things to those of you
who lack perception: like how to have fun at night,
like the time taking away from you the moments
it takes to know you have been passed over for
someone else. But you persist. Because you are cold,
because the skins, even the fur once wrapped around
you, is nowhere to be found. It is here that we learn
to love you: two faces, and therefore two minds,
resting between each other, even as the cold takes
away your breath.

3.

In time, you will need to give back your breath. In
time, you will want those you love by your side.
But before this, before you give back your breath,
you will need to say goodbye: to your beloved, to
the children you taught to climb each fence, to the
warmth of your own cheek. But there is a before-
this. Before this are the people you hope will precede
you; you hope to never feel their loss. People who
have held onto you because they could not walk
alone into night. They could mold the day into the
arms that pull them up and over their fear. But,
as the light changes, you need to be there before
darkness lays them down, rolls them over, and with
hands you cannot see, stops their breath.

PART II: GRAVITATIONAL WAVES

Something has to hold on, hold until you stay. Stay long enough to measure how far you are from the end, knowing, if you don't know where things fall, they land, often on their backs trying to breathe. What is inside you pulls out, misses the mark, misses all that comes after. When you try to grab hold, the center folds.

As you wait for your next breath, your next step, a hand to hold, a soft touch puts you to sleep. You are still finding your way to a child's kiss. Still, you have to find a way to hold on. You slip. You look inside of what drops you, dark with the holes opening inside. Still, you have something, and that something is the size of a guess.

You use this to get in over your head. Nevertheless, you try to lift yourself. You breathe. You stop. No one knows how you rest because you spin each side. It is the same forward as backward. Your violence surrounds you, to never change.

Swift migrations. Falling stars. Which begs the question, which lanes allow you to pass and which ones lead to a place for rest, what questions form the base of trust, and why do you keep arriving in the

wind? You stand between two hills. Several lanes
lead in each night; as many lead out.

The last time you looked, whole nights eaten by
cattle destroy the entire premise. Shade covers the
lanes between the trees and the leaves falling each
morning. You think moons in stillness, you think
each new turn on your way in, on your way out. You
are turning over because this side will not hold.

How you finally stand, how each life ends steadies
the bottom you drop down to what is said before
falling through the beginning of what is good and
right. You think another side will rise up to protect
all that you believe, and all that you believe stands
with you. Each lane between setting the sun beside
you.

This is where you now stand, in the last measure of
fairness waiting for the lines to be drawn through
the holes you walked for years, the sun beside you
burning through each lane, the waves you find
hiding the weight of a blessing and a curse, find the
lines that show you how fire begins, the ashes of
those who do not survive, and how you follow.

PART III: EQUIVALENCE

A.

4.

Before you know what the question is, ask of it: If
the leaves carry the known amount of weight in
some trees, and you wake up each morning unable
to move, do the hills binding you to the paths you
promised to follow, lean you over the turns in which
you lose control? And while at rest, does this interval
wait for you in the absence of light underneath?
Does this absence, waiting for the wind to begin,
gather along the edge you resemble? Before mass or
form, will all the weight pause before you?

3.

Lines to fish the crack along your crust stretches the
wake by which you arrive until you learn to lean in
each direction. Taking the corners too fast, shaving
off a part of you and the surfaces on which you begin
missing the breaks. Lost in the traffic you create. In
loneliness, searching for someone to drive next to
when traced carefully, a thin blue line sets the sky,
the forest beneath, the roads filling in your texture,
you form the intervals between.

2.

This time, you smell like steel. Just before the roads and the curves, winding through your descent, round your first wreck. You settle here, between loose leaves and fallen branches. Each lost leg hobbles over the gravel towards a night passing the wrong side of the road. A piece of sky falling over everything, turning the corner. You suspect that you are more than an idea at rest, an opening in the rock, where bones lie next to a thread of water. Fortunately, you hold on to the lights falling as nights collapse. Chipping stones to light a fire. You hear voices. At the back of the cave. You walk between shadows, setting yourself down in the darkness once lit by you.

1.

The moonlight falling guides you back into the trees. Away from your hands, still trying to steer. You think that possibly none of this happens: a blade of grass your hill folds neatly into your pocket as the sky around you flies off on wings whose hollow bones easily catch the wind, lifting you into a sky starting to burn across the weight you hold tightly in your arms, all life precious now, to remember how you begin, how you start slowly this time.

B.

4.

A struggle leans into the trees on a branch from
which to swing when the leaves no longer make
enough beds. You have slept here many nights. A
piece of advice, to help you slip through the leaves,
offers the reasons to choose which stretch of wind
to follow. You already know you must be careful;
too often the wrong intent veers across lines once
carefully drawn for your protection. Before these
lines, too much risk strayed from the safety of the
middle where calmer winds remained as long as the
first streaks of deception ran in place, staying away
from lies of omission and everything said behind
your back that has been known to harm. The safest
place on earth, once thought to exist only after
existence, becomes your approximation. So you
try to stay in the topmost leaves, where you can see
everything around you, especially that which keeps
to itself. Like the moss. Otherwise, too much stuff
will try to make its way in, take away the stalks to
build homes elsewhere. You know this because the
nights no longer keep a necessary quiet and you have
begun to bury your face into the crook of your arm
so as to not hear each piece dropping. Inevitably,
each piece dropped evokes the decisions whether to
stay. But this is your home. This is how you begin.
Your dream is to last here forever. This is a common
perspective. Nothing more.

3.

When the straps loosen around your face, and the mask comes off, what is left bends along the roads. Passing by a grove of trees, suffering the saw's first cut while other trees continue a straight line ahead of a better you. Standing inside our meadow, thin shadows paint the steps leading to a ledge just below your flock, lifting you away, lifting you into the face you remember once upon a time. A face that centers the rest of you, where confusion is all you really need to understand why one size dressed all you change, tell the story of each face ordained.*

2.

You stay close to the tree line, close to the bush birds fly from. When you do leave, it's to follow the elk as far as the roads, watch them cross in the middle of the night. Pick up their bodies, flying in and out of the glass. Here, you pull the skins across the roads each day. Fur hiding behind trees too thick to enter. The feet you never noticed squat down, wait for a pair of legs to enter. When night falls, it falls in place yet behind the steps, necessary to reach your breath. Someone walks beside you, peels away the remaining skin. Here is the muscle you count on. Lifting the car pinning you down is no small feat. And yet you find yourself back on top, holding everything you almost left behind, even the fear that remains just in case.

1.

The mane clutching your throat remains, keeps
everything warm and in place. The herds swim
into the trees on the other side, and the trees, by
themselves, lay down the ends that start over on a
common ground. Almost complete, beside the errors
you could not imagine. now permanently inside the
creeks, washing your sorrows a second time. All of us
need a second chance, nest carefully, one night only.

A.

4.

How long does it take to drive down a star about
to shine on the weight under the moon? Gives us
your only sister. You draw the lines, so we stay inside
you. You try to forget how hard your surface is,
how misguided your intentions. You believe we are
the ones hiding safely behind the trees inside your
meadow, yet we are only the bait left on the shore for
others to use, cast all lines further than the rest of us
sitting up straight, in front of the glass, turning on
the keys.

3.

You use the leaves in front of you to clean the
skins you try to save from burns spreading across
everyone. The hooks lining your lips, the paintings
hanging from your trees, the reasons you fall asleep
listening to the same sounds every night, sounds you
swear you will someday know how to share. Sounds
across the sky at the exact moment your life begins.
Hopefully, you will be at the head of the line, the
face smiling across from you, a different face than
the one gathering your veneer, each sheet bending
a memory, a recollection, a darkening road. Your
car taking a corner too fast until you bring yourself
form.

2.

To begin, you hang onto the air. You swing.
Everything swings back. You keep thinking if you
can swing far enough, you can put each piece back
where you begin. Each day you try on a new foot
so you can drive. You still think you can change the
ways you turn. Why you never see yourself drives
by. You try on new slips of paint. Still, you are rarely
seen. When you are young, everything is different.
You are a color just beginning. Everyone takes
notice. You watch yourself expand. When you are
big, we invite you into the front seat. Many of us will
stay interested in your time here.

1.

You tilt yet the water stays. You let us believe in the
trees you love. Their promise. Hooves arrive after.
You will be tall when the layers slide between. Each
time you are missing there is a correction, always
followed by the next error, fitting each together like
gloves placed carefully in your lap. Some small steps
follow you back, anything larger surely in danger of
being noticed. It is best you stay here for now, sitting
quietly with your hands folded. The last excuse
you use is not necessary; we all know the truth and
the consequences; we all prepare our schedules
together and will surely find each other. There are

days now you have the time to think about life itself, whom you will bump into and why. What is really confusing stretches further the ideas, trying so hard not to upset you by failing to resolve who is a good person. The idea that never considers itself for a moment, staying much too long with friends, talking long into the night, laughing together.

B.

4.

It will be enough to remember what happens, when
everything stays its clumsy course, and you poke
and prod to try and remember anything ever done
without you. There is something putting something
into the last time we are together. Perhaps it is
simply the tones of you arriving. We remember
you as a being so still, like a pond in the back of
your local library, and now you ripple, jump even,
like frogs hunting flies across hot stones. What
actually happens is each of us looks at the various
times we try to do our best, help anyone lagging
behind, making sure no one is left without a net
in which to fall, should an unexpected side shift
and the earth, taking a few moments to catch up,
shake uncontrollably, until everyone finds the
right doorway in which to stand. That none of
this happens without the cars bringing you here.
Bringing you to the signs before each curve instructs
you, do not pass. Bringing you to the herds right
before they leap. Bringing you hope. You can learn
again to stay completely still.

3.

The layers change each road you travel. One road on
top of the other. Same hill, same forest, same herd,

same meadow, same frozen lake, same fires drying
out the skins you try on, the same bodies on the side
of each road, even your car taking off. The corner
of your face pressed against the glass, against the
elk lying down, giving up its breath as you gather
yourself to drive the rest of us past our turn, as if, we
too, stay alive.

2.

Had you never left your hill, staying where the
leaves hide you, never finding the roads leading to
the one empty car waiting, and with enough gas
to drive to either side. Had you, like now, with no
family left, perhaps continued walking further and
further into the trees where no one finds you, where
there is enough water to keep moving, where you
realize what you really have to offer, and what turns
out to be truly important, finding us where we are
now, waiting for you to be more than your surface.
Something we can put our arms around, hold onto
when we feel there is nothing left to stand on, to
stop holding our breath, waiting again for the space
turning on the premise. No one dies there, that here
is a time where new life forms immediately after.

1.

It is not enough you know, more than anything

else, to drive ahead. The wrong car leaves you on the side of the road no one turns into. You have known forever how long it takes to drive home. You tell no one. At the same time, you see the clip clop, the piece almost at rest, prodding at such a pace no one can imagine missing you, should they throw right back the thread no one else remembers to bring along. The thread wraps around your hook, line, and sinker. Wraps around your finger. Helping you to remember the piece, forgetting nevertheless the stacks of clouds you promised us, to keep us here, waiting for the rain. Like you promised, the sharpest knife cuts us free. Like you promised, we see you clear as a bell, then you are gone. This is the way it works: forwards and backwards, backwards and forwards. A few cars spaced between.

PART IV:
COMPLEMENTARITY A

1.

Something is you and cannot be found. Each night
starting over, your slopes gathering together. You
slice your innocence, caress dead meat. You flash
your lights before each curve, a sign you are still
hoping to be found, each night starting over, looking
back to forget the other side of you, the inside of you
you do not understand, a light bending the poem
around you, a light bending you around us. When
your seams tear, you gather together all of your
cloth. You knit everything thin together. You knit
the skins lying on the side. You try knitting together
the blood remaining, you learn about the tar that
takes away your pain. You did not know the rip runs
through the left runs through the right, runs through
a chance for later.

1.

The moment before spreads across you. You want
your hill a little closer. Here, you are a shape that
lasts; an idea; buried under, a tautology; a pipe
bends a poem inside a jar inside a hill inside a jar.
This side of your road rounds the corner. What grass
lies down next to you? What do stars leave behind?
Will we meet a possibility? Shall we sit next to each
other? Our hands resting by our sides help us keep
to ourselves. In between never follows. The lights on
top shine after. Before we try to leave, you lean over,
help us out. You learn which streets, covered with
tents, sell you the tar with which to dream.

1.

It is like looking through the back of your head.
There, the elk swimming upstream protect their
young. You swim upstream to bring the rest of us
home. When there is wind, you open up your sails.
If all grows calm, you rest alone in blue waters. As
it should be. As if it is not the times everyone is
trying to forget, because home is now a tent, because
all of us lost know There may or may not last. We
watch you entering the tents buying the tar you
leave us before you disappear. As we end, you ask the
questions, "How?" and "Why?" There are those of
us who argue that the streets fill with tents so the elk
can find us, show us the water running through you.

1.

Here, the questions concerning your past are rarely
asked. You think you are a rose because you live in
the soil of flowers, useful when placed carefully in
each row. You, with your thorns tearing through
the mistakes you make, take it on the chin, leaning
against the ropes to open up the ring; the rest of us,
climbing onto the mat, knowing we could be next,
knowing each day is the same as before, waking on
the floor of your tent, melting the black tar in a
spoon, feeling the tip slowly enter.

1.

You miss the rest of us and, sometimes, we miss you.
You, always on the edge we give great thought to
avoid, waiting for us to climb up and over, answer all
of your questions. Like, why hot tar each morning?
Like, why do you hide on fifth street, when
everything is straight down; why do you become a
cliff when you do so well as a hill, and, finally, why
do you settle inside a tent next to a pipe when your
whole life is based now on the hope for a dream that
may never happen?

1.

Skinned by stone of Mr. Hill, bright as bougainvillea
branch, dark as Mr. Cliff's down, antlers rut the
jib in which we stand, the rest of you a thin skirt in
which you dance, a probable cause at rest until the
morning your smell enters our tents and we come
for you, take you to a bed of ice, where you learn to
freeze just before you begin to rot. Everywhere you
ripple, like water, like the canvas of a sail inside the
dreams inside your tent. Dropping your guard, you
learn to hide. You learn nothing grows if you bury
the spade. In very little time without you, our bodies
drift, a little to the left, you, a perfect curve strapped
to our back. Can you tell us what happens next?
The same as before? The part of you you do not
understand, left behind for us to find? Are we only
you when we dream? The tree, the nest, the slit of
light over the ice, a trace of memories only we recall;
kindness bringing a gentle touch, a gentle wind
across the scabs on your skin.

1.

We plant you firmly in the ground. When our fever
begins, when our breaks fail around the turn, the elk
leave the trees to cross. Time and time again we bury
you inside a ditch, inside a white boat burning where
you dream your last caress. Something has to hold
on to us until we stay. Something tries to get in over
our head, takes our steps away. A part of us, snipped,
falls to the side. A part of us leans over to kiss you a
final time. A part of us still believes we are walking
together, straight ahead, where the smallest children
grow, where the roots touch, calm our worst fears.
If you don't believe us, check your paintings you left
behind, check your ashes for the last time. When
you hear us, don't retreat, we are at the rear. We have
watched your shadows closely. When you decide to
leave, leave your decision behind. There are ways out.
But not with us.

1.

We imagine the water falling off of us, into you. The
steps you take rest on the soft hands you bury. You
forget the day it begins, and the closer we are tucks
in the corners, tucks in the sides. You recede in time,
walk into your tent, listen to the hooves of elk on
fifth street bringing with them the trees in which to
hide. We stand here, waiting. We stand here beside
you. You smell of black tar. Of pine. Of the metal
straps holding you in place holding your skin where
the needle pops your skin. In time, we walk away, we
find our meadow. This is us, a clearing of flowers. We
will never be you, once a hill with trees, with sides,
with roads around you. Your birds fill your clouds.
Should they need new nests, the birds join the elk.
As it should be. As if any of this around you is true.

1.

We are busy staying alive, ducking the conversation
beginning with, "It is what it is, don't worry,
tomorrow will be a new day; it is what it is." Buried
next to a leaky pipe bewilders. You are about to learn
all poems assemble through an illness only you can
dream. Try a pipe. We will. Never mind the blazing
sun. Lie down, buy a nickel bag. The herds breaking
through the trees barely survive. You know this. You
dream of a doe against your windshield. You raise
her calf on the side of you you do not understand.
Eventually, you give her our meadow. We love her
as our own. We give her our new grass, the pines to
protect her. Your last gift, the skins on the sides of
your roads to keep her warm.

1.

We are hungry and need water. We begin to dig
for roots. You walk into the sunlight. We stay. We
believe in you, in the branch you hover over the
earth. We know, if you have to, you will walk as far as
the green trees fall. We know you lie down at night
dreaming of the water just below your surface. We
know your fish will take your bait. So we seek refuge,
to lie down wherever the shade exists. We know our
flowers will die in front of us. For hope to exist, we
drive as far away as possible. We know, eventually,
we have to put on the breaks. We know this. We
also know, when your turn comes, you will barely
survive the crash. We have no idea how you became
ill. When we fall asleep, you leave. You drive far, all
the way to fifth street. You have hope the tar of your
dreams will bring you time. To survive this, we exist
on the other side. Each day we cross a new stream. If
you call our name, we come.

1.

Still, something enables you to stay in place. For a
moment it feels like the length of you. Then your
weight tries to find us. Your thought is we will
lighten your load. Your thought is you could be
elsewhere; you could even be something else, like
bait for the fish swimming ahead of you. Never
mind, we alone spread the ice over the corners,
tucking in the sides you no longer need, and now,
inside your dreams, fresh water flows; you climb
over us in your sleep; as your fevers begin, your skins
start to fold, one layer at a time. You appear like fresh
meat, actually, the scabs beneath.

1.

On the other side of you, everything the same as
before. Each night starting over, like you but on the
other side of you, never in the same skin, never at
the same time, yet at the same moment like a sun
setting each day. Like the elk who seem to know
where they're moving to as they're moving, the
same as your breath knowing to repeat once more.
Like the side of you you never knew before, a side
so steep you remain oblivious to its face even when
you are on it. Right now, you are trying to walk back
from your fever but feeling yourself sinking further
and further into the ice. That we love you needs no
explanation, that we now sweat in our own addiction
makes perfect sense considering who we are to each
other: no longer separate, no longer trying to find
each other when the breaks fail and the elk cross the
road. There is nothing mystical about it. We have
shared the same language for so long, pretending
an existence through suppositions and pronouns
will continue until recurrence stops forever the last
conversation in which we refer to each other in our
dreams.

1.

You write on the walls of your tent, instructing us
where we are to go and whom to follow. You write
what we will see after we arrive and what deserves
attention: the little boy wondering away from the
mission for sure, and if it is not in ash, the white
boat burning, perhaps a new way for everything that
needs to lie down, perhaps a way, finally, to grasp
how to think about all of this now rather than later
when you have grown too thin to lift the glass you
will have such trouble holding onto. A fever lasts and
lasts, and then you pass like cars lost between your
streets. Yet it takes such a long time for the sounds
that know you to fade, and the forms which you are
possibly capable of later to follow, when the people
closest to your heart fold into the flowers blooming
in the meadow you now share with us, and all that
lands forward gives birth to you again, the denied-
forever, your last fix finally able to let go of the fierce
grasp everything you thought of adhered to.

PART V:
COMPLEMENTARITY B

-1.

Neither you, nor anyone else, actually lies in the road
bleeding. Yet you are in the road, really in the road,
it's just that you, personally, have never actually been
there. You think you have, and you can still see the
blood on your hands as the sky shines elsewhere, the
water rising, catching itself on the lowest branch,
rising into the clouds, rain finally cleaning away your
presence, which is merely a reflection that appears
and disappears as we conceive of you, imagining us
after the dust cleans the lens looking down on the
old and lumpy chair in which you sit, believing you
are still the hill you have always thought yourself
to be, the roads around you actually leading us to
think of you as the glass shatters into the front seat
and the smallest of wings slice through you through
us. It never occurs to you there is a back seat. You
do remember someone mentioning it. That it is
especially nice for couples in the evenings when the
sun sets. That babies are often there in little seats
staring out the window. You are like that baby now.
Everything happening to you for the first time,
simply appearing as in a mirror, shining back, .

-1.

Now that you are merely the thoughts of a landscape,
you think carefully, ideas arise you never considered
letting anyone in on, like the reason to preserve the
seams of a horizon you sew together for us to have
a straight line on which to return. None of your
ducks are lining up as you thought, and only a tiny
aspect of us now tries to find the pocket into which
you fold each memory of a sky looking back at the
leaves falling when the wind decided to stop, when
the moon stayed even though you walked away from
a story you imagine whenever you need a moon, a
story everyone, inside their own moon, tells themself
to drag back the tide to step into the story each of us
fails to remember. A story in which you see yourself
looking at a poem looking back.

-1.

You never guess we are on the opposite side. Never
against you, always against you. You might suspect
this to be the case. We give you hints, intermittently,
but all the same, easily seen by anyone who cares to
look. Evidently, you never do, or can't, it all depends
on which side of the coin you stamp your hopes
to find us. You seem to want your efforts taken for
granted, which we do, and now, sitting where you
sit, unable to reach us, a sad place rests, looks after
you. You never dreamed of being so alone. Each
breath you take tries to find us, still, you reach for
the sky you haven't seen for years, ever really, because
the air you breathe is only in your dreams; we know
this because our soft touch is still ahead of you.
Never mind what comes; the penny you lay on the
tracks is for later; for now, you lean forward; the
rest of you arrives after we leave, after you pull back
your shoulders, stand straight, look ahead at what
follows; the space between us stops short of the time
allowed for time for you to appear, to keep yourself
as yourself, who you might become.

-1.

Your poetry will never reach as far as the wave, but
you and only you evolved to a story told by a distant
tree growing alone in the sea, its roots grabbing
onto the receding shore the moon of night and
day pull towards you. And you, your own branches
holding onto the tiny claws of a blackbird, looking
while being watched, spreading the thin mist of
your beginning and your end, as you begin again for
the last time. This is a matter of reflection, a state
not to be confused with looking inside the bowl
in which you understand what and which is being
poured into you; it's a state of understanding light
and dark, reaching you as the shadows on the walls
slowly crumbling, thin layers of your flesh laid across
the narrative that has, forever, written itself quietly
outside your comprehension, because, in the depths
of your grief, what needs to be told belongs to us,
a story we tell with great caution because of how
difficult it is to withstand so much disappointment,
because the story of regret can only be told to those
of us who feel regret, an imperative for any form of
decency, which, at last count, has slipped through so
many fingers there is now a shortage of hands.

-1.

You decide to take a stand. Right before our eyes. If
we can, we will help you to the corner of your hill
where you are last seen. After that, you're on your
own. Keep a light step as all of us nearby hope to
find you off guard, vulnerable to the light we leave
behind each time we disappear. The catch to which
you are accustomed each evening depends on the
swells each day as well as the time it takes you to sail
into the beds of kelp that feed you. Eidetic by most
standards, but always behind the scenes spilling over
the sides you can and cannot see, your only wish now
is for someone to follow you up and over, bringing
the moments that prove you are still here and why.
Turn off the lights; let the ants discover the crumbs
on the floor. Prepare your sponge; wipe away all
you can and cannot see. You remember exactly what
happened that night, where you might have been
and why you seem to still be there.

-1.

In the shade each thought spreads, you leave behind
each reason to set things straight, leave behind the
same reason you continue to walk into thin air, the
reason stars vanish or an instance occurs. In the
time it takes to turn your head, the water left behind
dries beneath your eyes. You start the wind, try to
believe in someone else, perhaps detect the breath
that follows. For now it is make-believe, as if, while
listening for the moment each of us returns, every
step lifts the seconds in which we predict how you
appear and disappear, how you come up for air,
descend into dark waters. As you turn off our lights,
we turn the corner. You are here, sitting on the side
of the road waiting to cross. You are here, sitting in
the front seat. You are here, your antlers brushing
against your trees, brushing against any trace of you.
When we find you, we check each other's wounds.
If either of us walk away, the trees follow. Then the
elk. Then the meadow. Then the hill. The last time
we see you, we ask for something of yours to carry us
through. It is easy to forget each other. Thankfully,
there are places each of us know to find the other
after dark. Where the wind dies down. Where we
left our scent.

-1.

In truth, all of us return every moment lifts a finger, a
thin rope with a barb perfectly stringing together our
lips, each of us hanging in the hot air, a split second
later falling short, a disappointment reconciled
for the first and last time. You see yourself in us as
we do in you, a curious mix of hopes and dreams,
misunderstandings, regrets at having so much pain
left on the boards of a pier that stopped short of the
sand sifting through your hands holding down the
lines, the hooks cast out late into the night. As far
as you know, everything is going fine; the last time
you looked, a precarious and significant amount
of weight is left to deal with, will wait until later. A
scary thought, holding itself back because none of us
will be here to remember, is of you after all, is of us
to begin with, because each time one of us starts to
think of the other, one of us drifts further off.

-1.

There are ways to stay in view, falling down one of them, disappearing so we miss you another. There are ways to keep this up. There are ways to lose your taste, your smell, reduce the time in which you pass by; the ships arriving carry the sick at your command; everyone with orders to stay on deck washes into the sea, relieved at the chance to swim for shore. You remember us clearly. We are the clearing you made for us halfway up your hill; we are the flowers living and dying in your rain, your sunlight, your hope to grow as far as your first turn, planting ourselves on the edge. Which side you face folds for the last time, the last time filled with your hope for us. That we no longer find you deserves a pause. We will wait here. We know you will return. You always have. When you return, wear your mask. It is easier to see underneath you, where you stand, before your first step.

-1.

You come right up to our skin and through it. A
side to you lies down for the side of you that gets
back up. For so many years, you think you are a hill.
You fall in love with moonlight. You think you are
finally rising. You think we are happy as the meadow
below you. You wave from the clouds. Suddenly you
wake in a cave. Suddenly you wake on the side of a
road, holding your sister in your arms. You weep.
Days and nights pass, your beloved moon rising only
to disappear. The math changes and you, merely a
reflection of what can go wrong, go wrong. Your
breath slowly leaves you. You come right up to our
skin and through it. In a warm room, the air around
you turns to ice. The birds you think are always here
fly there. What is finally possible looks over your
equation. Approves. You get it right.

ALSO OUT ON FAR WEST

SONNY VINCENT......................................Snake Pit Therapy

BRENT L. SMITH....................................Pipe Dreams on Pico

JOSEPH MATICK..The Baba Books

KURT EISENLOHR..Stab the Remote

KANSAS BOWLING..................A Cuddly Toys Companion

KANSAS BOWLING & PARKER LOVE BOWLING...................
......................Prewritten Letters for Your Convenience

CRAIG DYER..............Heavier Than a Death in the Family

PARKER LOVE BOWLING............Rhododendron, Rhododendron

JENNIFER ROBIN...............You Only Bend Once with a
......................................Spoonful of Mercury

JOSEPH MATICK..Cherry Wagon

RICHARD CABUT......................................Disorderly Magic

NORMAN DOUGLAS...............Love and the Fear of Love

ELIZABETH ELLEN..Estranged

JEFFREY WENGROFSKY.............The Wolfboy of Rego Park

HAKON ADALSTEINSSON........................Our Broken Land

A FAR WEST ANTHOLOGY........................Pretty Obscure

LILY LADY..NDA

NIKOLA PEPERA........................Lay Down & Get Lost

JACK SKELLEY..Myth Lab

PETER CROWLEY..Down at Max's

STEVE KRAKOW.............A Mind Blown Is A Mind Shown

ADDISON FULTON..Social Animals

TONY O'NEILL..Forged Prescriptions

CYNTHIA ROSS..The Secret Door

farwestpress.com
+1 (541) FAR-WEST

www.ingramcontent.com/pod-product-compliance
Lightning Source LLC
Chambersburg PA
CBHW020754130626
46554CB00006B/2179